Sports Idols™

TIGER WOODS

Jason Glaser

PowerKiDS press.

New York

To the Borkowskis, who (sometimes) keep a straight face when I tee off

Published in 2008 by The Rosen Publishing Group, Inc.
29 East 21st Street, New York, NY 10010

First Edition

Editor: Amelie von Zumbusch
Book Design: Julio Gil
Photo Researcher: Nicole Pristash

Photo Credits: Cover, pp. 5, 7, 9, 11, 13, 15, 17, 19, 21 © Getty Images; cover (golf ball) Shutterstock.com.

Library of Congress Cataloging-in-Publication Data

Glaser, Jason.
  Tiger woods / Jason Glaser. — 1st ed.
      p. cm. — (Sports idols)
  Includes index.
  ISBN 978-1-4042-4179-4 (lib. bdg.)
  1. Woods, Tiger—Juvenile literature. 2. Golfers—United States—Biography—Juvenile literature. I. Title.
  GV964.W6G53 2008
  796.352092—dc22
  [B]
                              2007020931

Manufactured in the United States of America

SPORTS IDOLS

21.25/15.85 ea. All 6 for 127.50/95.10

Accelerated Reader Disk: AR Quizzes available

This high-interest series for young readers profiles six of today's most exciting athletes. Each book traces a sport star's career from childhood through the current day.

Rosen/PowerKids, Grades 2-5, 2008, 24 Pages, 8" x 8", color photos, index, glossary

DANICA PATRICK - Jason Glaser
DAVID BECKHAM - Jason Glaser
MARIA SHARAPOVA - Jason Glaser
TIGER WOODS - Jason Glaser
TIM DUNCAN - Jason Glaser
TOM BRADY - Jason Glaser

Contents

Becoming the Best

Today, Tiger Woods is the world's best-known golfer. As a boy, Tiger kept a timeline on his wall tracking the life of **professional** golfer Jack Nicklaus. Many people thought Nicklaus was the greatest golfer ever. Tiger's timeline showed how old Nicklaus was when he won each match, or game. Tiger wanted to do everything Nicklaus had done earlier than Nicklaus did it.

Woods is on his way to accomplishing this. So far, he has won four Masters' **tournaments** to Nicklaus's six. Woods broke many golf records set by Nicklaus. Now many people think Woods is the greatest golfer in the world.

Woods and Jack Nicklaus are friends today. Nicklaus thinks Woods is a great player. He said of Woods, "I would be very surprised if he doesn't break my records."

Born to Play Golf

Earl and Kutilda Woods's son, Eldrick, was born on December 30, 1975. Earl gave Eldrick the nickname Tiger, after a Vietnamese soldier. The soldier had saved Earl's life when he was fighting in the **Vietnam War**.

Tiger was less than a year old when he took his first golf swing. He had watched Earl hit many golf balls into a net at the Woods's Cypress, California, home. Tiger stood by a ball with a small club his dad gave him. To his parents' surprise, Tiger hit the ball right into the net over and over.

Tiger Woods's parents gave him a rich cultural background. Woods is part African American, part Asian, part white, and part Native American.

Tiger Wins Early

Even as a kid, Tiger was a great golfer. He won his first **Junior** World Cup tournament at 8 years old. When he was 12, Tiger won all 30 tournaments he entered.

Tiger's father taught him about mind games. He made noises when Tiger swung, but Tiger learned not to listen. At 15, Tiger's strong mind helped him become the youngest person to win the U.S. Junior **Amateur** prize. When he was in high school, Tiger won six big **championships**. After high school, Tiger went to Stanford **University**. There, he won nine tournaments and became NCAA Player of the Year.

In 1992, Woods took part in his first PGA, or Professional Golf Association, event. He was such a good amateur that he got permission to play at the Los Angeles Open.

A Fast Start

At Stanford, Woods won the U.S. Amateur prize a record three times. At this time, more people watched Woods on television than watched pro, or professional, golfers! Tiger Woods knew it was time for him to become a professional, too. He turned professional the day after winning his third amateur trophy, or prize.

Woods needed to either win a lot of money or win one tournament to play in the big tournaments the next year. If he did not, he would go to a school for new pros. Luckily, Woods won two of the seven tournaments in which he took part!

In August 1996, Tiger Woods took part in the Greater Milwaukee Open. It was his first event as a professional golfer.

Among the Masters

Woods won four PGA Tour events his first year. His greatest win was at the 1997 Masters Tournament. He set a record for the lowest score for a Masters Tournament. Woods won the tournament by 12 **strokes**, which was also a record.

The Masters is one of four **major** golf tournaments. Winning all four in one year is called a grand slam. In 2000, Woods won the U.S. Open, the British Open, and the PGA Championship. In 2001, he won the Masters. Woods was the first person to be the champion of all four at once. People called this the Tiger Slam.

As all Masters Tournament winners do, Woods received a special green jacket. Nick Faldo, who had won the tournament the year before, helped Woods put on the jacket.

Playing Through Pain

Woods's left knee started to hurt while he played. He began playing poorly in major tournaments. Woods had already had knee **surgery** when he was at Stanford, but his knee was troubling him again. In 2002, Woods had another knee operation. The operation helped, but Woods could not swing his golf club the same way anymore.

Woods needed to learn a new golf swing. He had to practice more than ever to forget his old swing. Woods asked a new golf coach, or teacher, to help him. Woods worked hard and won three of his first four tournaments after the surgery.

Tiger Woods took part in the Buck Invitational just a few months after his knee surgery. He surprised many people when he won the tournament by four strokes!

Tiger Today

Woods wanted to be the best again. In 2005, Woods won the Masters and the British Open. These were his first major wins in three years. In 2006, he won the British Open and the PGA Championship. Woods took back the number-one ranking that year.

As 2007 began, Woods had 12 major wins and 54 total PGA wins. Still, there were things Woods had yet to do. He had never come from behind to win a major tournament. At the 2007 Masters, Woods took the lead in the last round. He kept it a short time but ended up in second place.

Tiger Woods almost always plays with Steve Williams as his caddy. A caddy carries a golfer's golf clubs. Woods always uses a stuffed tiger cover named Frank on his clubs.

17

More to Life than Golf

While golfing, Woods tries to stay away from traps called water hazards. Off the golf course, Woods loves the water. He has a 155-foot (47 m) boat he uses for diving, fishing, and traveling. Woods named the boat **Privacy** because he can hide from cameras on it.

Woods visits *Privacy* with his wife, Elin. Elin Nordegren was a nanny for one of Woods's golf friends. The two met at the British Open in 2001. They started dating and married in 2004. In June 2007, their daughter, Sam, was born. Woods was very happy to be a father. Sadly, he could not share his joy with his own father, who had died the year before.

Elin and Tiger Woods also like other sports besides golf.
Here they are watching a tennis match in 2006.

Giving Back

Tiger Woods began helping others when he was young. During his first trip to the Masters, in 1995, Woods ran a clinic, or lessons, for Augusta National's African-American **caddies**. Augusta is where the Masters takes place. Woods knew that no one else would teach the caddies.

Woods understood that he was lucky to have parents who helped and stood by him. He knew that many other kids could not follow their dreams. Woods started the Tiger Woods **Foundation** in 1996. His foundation gives golf clinics to inner-city youth. It also gives money to children who need help reaching their dreams.

Tiger Woods founded the Tiger Woods Learning Center, in Anaheim, California, to help kids in school and at golf. He took part in the groundbreaking on April 16, 2003.

Tiger Woods in the Years to Come

Tiger Woods set out to beat every record in golf. He has already broken many of the records that were listed on the timeline on his childhood wall. Woods practices hard and has no plans to slow down. Someday, he could win more Masters and major tournaments than anyone in golf history. He has already become the youngest person to win all four majors.

Golf is changing to handle Tiger Woods. Courses like Augusta are making their grounds longer and narrower. Some call these changes Tiger-proofing. Even so, Woods will likely show that no course is safe from him.

Glossary

amateur (A-muh-tur) Having to do with someone who does something without pay.

caddies (KA-deez) People who carry a golfer's bag on a golf course.

championships (CHAM-pee-un-ships) Events held to decide the best, or the winner.

foundation (fown-DAY-shun) A group set up to give help for a cause.

junior (JOON-yor) Having to do with young people.

major (MAY-jur) Very important.

privacy (PRY-vuh-see) The freedom to be alone and not watched.

professional (pruh-FESH-nul) Someone who is paid for what he or she does.

strokes (STROHKS) Swings to hit a golf ball.

surgery (SER-juh-ree) An operation.

tournaments (TOR-nuh-ments) Groups of games to decide the best player.

university (yoo-neh-VER-seh-tee) A school one goes to after high school.

Vietnam War (vee-it-NOM WOR) A war fought between South Vietnam and North Vietnam, from 1954 to 1975, in which America fought.

Index

Web Sites

Due to the changing nature of Internet links, PowerKids Press has developed an online list of Web sites related to the subject of this book. This site is updated regularly. Please use this link to access the list: www.powerkidslinks.com/sidol/tiger/